Reflections

Seasons of comfort and joy

Meditations in verse based on select Scripture readings

Anne Standfield

DayOne

© Day One Publications 2008
First Edition 2008

Unless otherwise indicated, Scripture quotations in this publication are from The New International Version, copyright ©1973, 1978, 1984, International Bible Society. Used by permission of Hodder and Stoughton, a member of the Hodder Headline Group. All rights reserved.

British Library Cataloguing in Publication Data available

ISBN 978-1-84625-103-0

Published by Day One Publications
Ryelands Road, Leominster, HR6 8NZ

☎ 01568 613 740
FAX: 01568 611 473
email—sales@dayone.co.uk
web site—www.dayone.co.uk

Designed by Wayne McMaster and printed by Gutenberg Press, Malta

Dedication

This work is dedicated to the glory of God, my Lord and Saviour.

With thanks to Robin and Martin for their support and patience throughout the production of this work and to those who spurred me on to share the gift within me with those further afield, to the glory of God's name.

Contents

Author's note

God's Word, the Bible, is the guidebook to life for all people. Described in a term originating from the root word meaning 'reed', which was used as a form of measurement in biblical times, the canon of Scripture is the 'measuring rod' or standard by which we live out our lives before God, the Creator of all things. In it, God reveals himself to us and teaches us about ourselves and the world around us.

But how can sinful, rebellious people ever be reconciled to a holy God? Only the Bible has the answer! God longs to have a personal relationship with each of us and he has made this possible through the person and work of his one and only Son, Jesus Christ. Unless we have a right view of God and of our standing before him as individuals, we can never enter into a right relationship with him. God's Word is vital in revealing the truth to each and every one of us.

The poems contained within this book have been based solely upon Scripture with the aim that each reader may come to know the only true God and Jesus Christ, his Son, whom he has sent as our Saviour. This is the only way to eternal life (John 17:3). As an aid to this, I have listed the Scriptures from which each poem is inspired and would encourage you to read and meditate upon these Scriptures in order to obtain a fuller appreciation of the message of the poems.

Foundations

Carried

[Based on Isaiah 46:3–5.]

O God of all strength,
    Who is like unto you?
He who bears us from birth
    And will carry us through;
He who shines in our darkness,
    Brings us hope in despair,
In whose arms we are resting;
    Who with you can compare?

Isaiah 46:4:
'… I have made you and I will carry you; I will sustain you and I will rescue you.'

Eternal mystery

[Based on Ephesians 1:7–14.]

Oh, the riches of God's grace,
    Lavished all on me,
In making known his wondrous plan—
    His eternal mystery!
For in the purpose of his will
    He chose me in his Son;
My heart now sings his glorious praise
    For all that he has done!

Ephesians 1:11–12:
'In him we were also chosen, having been predestined according to the plan of him who works out everything in conformity with the purpose of his will, in order that we, who were the first to hope in Christ, might be for the praise of his glory.'

Faultless

[Based on Jude 24–25.]

Oh, what a glorious truth is this!
    What a wondrous thought!
That Christ, the only Saviour,
    To God's lofty throne has brought
Rebellious sinners, such as us,
    From rags to riches dressed,
Presents us there with greatest joy
    Clothed in his righteousness!
Oh, who can fathom all his ways?
    Explain his strange design?
For there we stand without a fault,
    Secured by grace divine!

Jude 24–25:
'To him who is able to keep you from falling and to present you before his glorious presence without fault and with great joy—to the only God our Saviour be glory, majesty, power and authority, through Jesus Christ our Lord, before all ages, now and for evermore! Amen.'

Grace alone

[Based on Ephesians 2:6–9.]

Saved by grace divine, through faith,
    God's gift to us is given;
Raised up on high with Christ our Lord,
    We're seated now in heaven.
        His grace shown to the uttermost—
        With nothing of ourselves to boast!

Ephesians 2:6–7:
'And God raised us up with Christ and seated us with him in the heavenly realms in Christ Jesus, in order that in the coming ages he might show the incomparable riches of his grace, expressed in his kindness to us in Christ Jesus.'

Hope of glory

[Based on Colossians 1:25–27.]

Christ in you, the hope of glory,
Fullness of the Father's Word;
Mystery hidden, now disclosing,
    Revealed to us in Christ the Lord:
Glorious riches here cascade
To show God's love to us displayed.

Colossians
1:27:
  'To them God has chosen to make known among the Gentiles the glorious riches of this mystery, which is Christ in you, the hope of glory.'

Morningsong

[Based on 1 Corinthians 1:21–25.]

God's 'foolishness' is wise,
His 'weakness' now made strong,
Surpassing all intelligence
    That unto men belong;
For by his grace alone
Christ crucified makes known
Through preaching of his powerful Word—
    Redemption's morningsong!

1 Corinthians
1:21:
  'For since in the wisdom of God the world through its wisdom did not know him, God was pleased through the foolishness of what was preached to save those who believe.'

Rich dwellings

[Based on Colossians 3:16–17.]

Let the Word of God dwell richly
In your heart, your tongue, your ways,
Teaching all with heavenly wisdom,
Singing songs of grateful praise.
  Whate'er you do in word or deed
  Do all for Christ—'tis joy indeed!

Colossians 3:16:
'Let the word of Christ dwell in you richly as you teach and admonish one another with all wisdom, and as you sing psalms, hymns and spiritual songs with gratitude in your hearts to God.'

Set free

[Based on Romans 8:1–2.]

No condemnation!' I hear that happy sound!
  For where my sin has reigned, God's grace does far abound;
Eternal life is mine, for Christ has borne my sin,
  Nailed it to his cross of shame and made me pure within.
Who, then, can raise a charge? Who brings a guilty plea,
  Since Christ, my sinless Saviour, died on Calvary for me?

Romans 8:1–2:
'Therefore, there is now no condemnation for those who are in Christ Jesus, because through Christ Jesus the law of the Spirit of life set me free from the law of sin and death.'

Stand steadfast

[Based on 1 John 3:2; 1 Corinthians 13:12.]

S tand steadfast in the Saviour:
The best is yet to come;
We know not now what we shall be
In our eternal home.
But this we know: when Christ appears
All shrouded mists will disappear
And everything will be made clear.

1 John 3:2:
'Dear friends,
now we are
children of God,
and what we
will be has not
yet been made
known. But we
know that when
he appears, we
shall be like him,
for we shall see
him as he is.'

Standing firm

[Based on Psalm 33:10–11.]

O f all the wondrous plans of God,
Not one shall move or fail;
Upheld by his almighty power,
There's none that's weak or frail.
Wrought in the realms of heaven above,
Eternal they all stand;
Unchanged by man, or time, or will,
Fulfilled as God has planned.

Psalm 33:11:
'But the plans
of the Lord stand
firm for ever, the
purposes of his
heart through all
generations.'

Timed to perfection

[Based on Habakkuk 2:3–4.]

The end from the beginning
    Is known unto the Lord,
And in his perfect timing
      His plans, they stand assured;
For though to us, things linger,
      Remaining unfulfilled,
The Lord has his appointed times
      When doubts and fears are stilled.
His sovereignty, it reigns supreme
      In every circumstance and scheme.

Habakkuk 2:3:
  'For the revelation awaits an appointed time; it speaks of the end and will not prove false. Though it linger, wait for it; it will certainly come and will not delay.'

Very essence

[Based on Philippians 2:6–11.]

God of God, alone,
    In very essence, he,
Creator all—above, beneath—
      Has donned humanity.
Who, in his humble death,
      The Father's will obeyed;
Now sits exalted on his throne—
      Redemption's price is paid!

Philippians 2:8–9:
  'And being found in appearance as a man, he humbled himself and became obedient to death—even death on a cross! Therefore God exalted him to the highest place and gave him the name that is above every name ...'

Watching

[Based on 1 Peter 5:10–11.]

Within your world of testings,
When sorrow paves the way,
The God of grace, who called you
To his eternal day,
Will lift you up, restore you,
Will make you strong and firm,
Will lead you in his steadfast path,
Will all his ways affirm.
For his is the eternal power
That watches o'er you every hour.

1 Peter 5:10–11:
'And the God of all grace, who called you to his eternal glory in Christ, after you have suffered a little while, will himself restore you and make you strong, firm and steadfast. To him be the power for ever and ever. Amen.'

Word incarnate

[Based on John 1:1–4,12–14, 18.]

Eternal realms, eternal Word,
Made man with men to dwell,
Was clothed in our humanity—
God's Son, Immanuel.
Through manhood, full of grace and truth,
The Father he has shown;
In Him is life, the light of men,
Revealing truths unknown:
For all who on his Name believe
Shall everlasting life receive.

John 1:14:
'The Word became flesh and made his dwelling among us. We have seen his glory, the glory of the One and Only, who came from the Father, full of grace and truth.'

Seasons

Autumnal

[Based on Romans 1:20.]

Autumnal colours all around—
Nature's richer shades—
Showing forth creation's sounds
In fields and everglades;
God's glory then is here displayed
Without a single word;
Just see the wonders of his hand—
The great Creator God.

Romans 1:20:
'Since the creation of the world God's invisible qualities—his eternal power and divine nature—have been clearly seen, being understood from what has been made, so that men are without excuse.'

Days of praise

[Based on Psalm 113:3.]

Sun-kissed beaches, golden, gleaming,
Wispy clouds seen floating by;
See, away on the horizon
Sinks the sun from azure sky.
See those colours there displaying
As the sunset ends its blaze;
Sing, my soul, with every other,
Give its Maker all your praise!

Psalm 113:3:
'From the rising of the sun to the place where it sets, the name of the Lord is to be praised.'

Daystar

[Based on Revelation 22:16.]

The lengthening of days and the
    shortening of nights,
    Reversal of yonder celestial lights,
The day has arisen to show unto all
    Dominion of light over darkest nightfall.
God's Daystar arises within every heart
    To shine on forever, and ne'er to depart;
Sin's darkness he cleanses and evil dispels
    In every believer whose heart he indwells.

Revelation 22:16:
'I, Jesus … am the Root and the Offspring of David, and the bright Morning Star.'

Eternal Lamb

[Based on Isaiah 53:6.]

The eternal Lamb of God
    Has shed his precious blood
To bring the wanderers to the fold
    And lead us back to God.
So raise salvation's song
    To realms beyond the sky;
For God's own Son has sacrificed
    His life, that sin may die!

Isaiah 53:6:
'We all, like sheep, have gone astray, each of us has turned to his own way; and the Lord has laid on him the iniquity of us all.'

Everglow

[Based on Malachi 4:2.]

The sinking summer sun lies low
  Within the twilight sky,
Gently bowing sleepy head,
    Leaves its domain on high;
But deep within my soul there lies
    God's Sun of Righteousness,
Which ne'er shall set; shall I forget
    My Saviour's faithfulness?

Malachi 4:2:
'But for you
who revere my
name, the sun
of righteousness
will rise with
healing in its
wings.'

Glorious day

[Based on John 8:12.]

Frosty ice and wintry winds,
  The darkness of the night,
Will all give way to glorious day
    When warmth reigns with the light.
Just as the cold and darkness flee
    And warmer days have come,
Sin's darkness will flee when Jesus we see,
    The Eternal Light, God's only Son.

John 8:12:
'[Jesus] said:
"I am the light
of the world.
Whoever follows
me will never
walk in darkness,
but will have the
light of life."'

Rising

[Based on 1 Peter 3:18; John 12:24.]

1 Peter 3:18:
'For Christ
died for sins
once for all, the
righteous for
the unrighteous,
to bring you to
God.'

A grain of wheat falls into the ground
And dies, new fruit to bring;
And in its dying, life is given—
A truly wondrous thing!
And Christ has died that he might give
Eternal life to all
Who love his Name and keep his ways,
Obedient to his call.

Showers

[Based on Psalm 72:6–7.]

Psalm 72:6–7:
'He [the king]
will be like
rain falling on
a mown field,
like showers
watering the
earth. In his days
the righteous
will flourish;
prosperity will
abound till the
moon is no
more.'

Showers of refreshing
Fall gently all around,
Kissing dell and everglade,
Revitalizing ground;
Refreshing showers of blessing
Fall gently on my soul,
For Christ has died, the crucified,
To make this sinner whole!

Summer's seal

[Based on Jeremiah 8:20.]

Jeremiah 8:20:
'The harvest is
past, the summer
has ended,
and we are not
saved.'

Come, gather the yield
Of orchard and field,
The harvest is past and the summer is sealed;
Be thankful, my heart,
And set time apart
To give honour to God for the love he's revealed.

Unfurled

[Based on 1 John 5:11.]

1 John 5:11:
'God has given
us eternal life,
and this life is in
his Son.'

The sleepy bud and blossom
From wintry slumber stir
To greet the glorious dawning
Of Springtide in the air;
Such beauteous shades unfolding,
All sprinkled with the dew,
Such wonder we're beholding,
At God's creation, new!

Whiter than snow

[Based on Psalm 51:7.]

Psalm 51:7:
*'... wash me,
and I shall be
whiter than
snow.'*

Glancing around, a blanket of white
Glistens and gleams in the mellow sunlight;
Silent it lies, untouched by man's hand,
A cloak of perfection now covers the land.
Yet God has a covering for sin to bestow—
A covering far better, far whiter than snow—
Righteousness' cloak to give every one
Who believes in his Word and accepts his dear Son.

By atonement

[Based on Ephesians 2:8–9; Hebrews 9:14–15.]

By atonement, not attainment,
Have I come unto this place;
By atonement, not attainment,
Brought before the throne of grace.
> Never merit of my own
> Could for all my sin atone;
> 'Tis Jesus' work, and his alone,
> By saving grace.

By atonement, not attainment!
Nothing could I ever plead,
Save the work of Christ, my Saviour,
For his Name is all I need;
> Nothing could I ever bring
> To the feet of God, my King—
> Christ gave for me his everything—
> His Name I plead.

Ephesians 2:8–9:
'For it is by grace you have been saved, through faith—and this not from yourselves, it is the gift of God—not by works, so that no one can boast.'

Continuance

[Based on 2 Timothy 3:14–17.]

From God-breathed sacred writings,
  Penned so long ago,
That you have known from infancy
    Continue then to grow.
For in salvation's pathway,
    God's wisdom you will learn;
And you can follow in his ways,
    His purposes discern.

Continue in that pathway
    And daily learn of him
Through his own sacred writings
    That wash you from your sin;
For they will train in righteousness,
    Will teach, rebuke, correct,
Equip you then for all good work,
    Your Saviour to reflect.

What you have learned unto this day
    Continue to increase,
That you may grow in godliness
    And know your Saviour's peace.
So as you walk God's pathway here,
    Attend unto his Word;
Be wise unto salvation
    Through faith in Christ, the Lord.

2 Timothy 3:14–17:
'But as for you, continue in what you have learned and have become convinced of, because you know those from whom you learned it, and how from infancy you have known the holy Scriptures, which are able to make you wise for salvation through faith in Christ Jesus. All Scripture is God-breathed and is useful for teaching, rebuking, correcting and training in righteousness, so that the man of God may be thoroughly equipped for every good work.'

Departure

[Based on Philippians 1:21–24.]

When I depart this earthly scene
And reach that golden shore,
Do not weep and mourn for me,
For I'm where I have longed to be,
    Where tears shall be no more.

When I depart this earthly scene
And tears, perhaps, shall fall,
Although my face you cannot see
I live there in your memory,
    My faith then to recall.

When I depart this earthly scene,
Remember, I am free
From all the pain that dwells within,
From all the burden of my sin;
    There nothing touches me.

When I depart this earthly scene,
How can you but rejoice?
While looking on my Saviour's face—
The One who's filled me with his grace—
    I'll hear his blessèd voice.

When I depart, I'll be with him,
His wondrous love retrace;
I'll praise his Name for evermore
Over on that heavenly shore,
    My final resting place.

Philippians 1:21–24:
'For to me, to live is Christ and to die is gain. If I am to go on living in the body, this will mean fruitful labour for me. Yet what shall I choose? I do not know! I am torn between the two: I desire to depart and be with Christ, which is better by far; but it is more necessary for you that I remain in the body.'

Exaltation

[Based on Psalm 145:1–3; Luke 22:19.]

Come, let us raise our praises high,
As round Christ's Name we gather,
Proclaiming all the worthiness of him upon the throne;
Come, let us raise our praises high,
Ascending to the Father,
Exalt Christ's Name high over all, his Holy Name alone.

For as we gather to his Name,
We contemplate his Being,
We ponder all the aspects of the Holy Son of God;
And as we gather to that Name,
All other thoughts are fleeing,
Save those of him, our Saviour, and the lonely path he
trod.

None other here is worthy found
Save Jesus, our own Saviour;
None other can fulfil the great demands that meet sin's
needs;
Just he alone is worthy found,
Commanding God's own favour,
This Jesus, who is perfect in his thoughts, his ways, his
deeds.

So let us raise our praises high
To him who brought salvation,
    To him who paid sin's price by shedding blood
      upon the tree;
Come now and let our praises rise
From every tongue and nation,
    Rise upwards to the Father's throne for all
      eternity.

Psalm 145:3:
*'Great is the
Lord and most
worthy of praise;
his greatness no
one can fathom.'*

Finer than gold

[Based on Psalm 19:7–11.]

These golden years have quickly flown,
With many memories,
But, oh, how precious they've become
In making them our own;
They've drawn us closer day by day,
As year succeeded year,
Much richer has our love become,
Grown deeper all the way.

Standing beyond the finest gold
Of love-rich memories,
A thing more precious, purer still,
Than aught our lives can hold;
For deep within our being lies
The tender love of God;
His law is written on our hearts:
This makes the simple wise.

Desire those wondrous truths of God,
Those purer, better paths—
Of sweeter taste than honeycomb—
    That saints of old have trod.
Desire God's precious, treasured Word
That leads us unto him;
Those finer, purer, golden words
    As spoken by our Lord.

More precious than the gold, so fine,
That's passed through human hands;
More precious than our memories,
    Down through the years of time.
Truth of our God, Redeemer, Lord,
That's held within our hearts;
And through his tender, keeping power
    Ours is the great reward.

Psalm 19:9–10:
*'The fear
of the Lord is
pure, enduring
for ever. The
ordinances of
the Lord are sure
and altogether
righteous.
They are more
precious than
gold, than much
pure gold; they
are sweeter than
honey, than
honey from the
comb.'*

Golden ways

[Based on Job 23:10–12; 1 Peter 1:6–7.]

The pathway of life you have travelled together
Down through the years, never turning aside,
Walking in steps that were made for each other,
Ordered by God as your heavenly Guide;
Following closely the way of his making,
Looking to him for his guidance to lead,
Fully entrusting the way you were taking,
Waiting on him to supply every need.

When on that pathway the dark clouds would gather—
Light is diminished! The way made obscure!—
Upwards you've looked to your heavenly Father,
Who, in his mercy, his love has assured.
Leading you on in the light of his presence,
Tenderly watching each step you have trod;
Gladly you've followed with firm acquiescence,
Knowing no harm would befall you, from God.

Testings have come oft without understanding,
    Causing some fear and the doubts to set in,
Yet, through his grace, he's enabled withstanding,
    Giving you peace and contentment within;
Deep is the trust you have placed in your Saviour,
    Knowing the truth that his way is the best;
Standing so firm in his Word, without waver,
    In calm, sweet assurance of his love possessed.

As you walk on in the way of his making—
    Traced out by God and by his hand controlled—
Know in your hearts that the way you are taking
    Will bring you both forth as pure, refined gold;
Testings that come, they, in glory, are showing
    Honour to God and a faith ringing true;
The wealth of faith's triumph surpasses all knowing
    And brings forth the praise that to his Name is due.

Job 23:10–12:
*'But he knows
the way that I
take; when he
has tested me,
I shall come
forth as gold.
My feet have
closely followed
his steps; I have
kept to his way
without turning
aside. I have not
departed from
the commands
of his lips; I
have treasured
the words of his
mouth more than
my daily bread.'*

In the midst

[Based on Matthew 18:20.]

Matthew 18:20:
'For where two
or three come
together in my
name, there am I
with them.'

Put Christ in the midst of your new life together,
Let him take control and he'll guide you for ever.
Put Christ in the midst and there let him preside,
    He'll lead you both forward, your footsteps to guide.

Put Christ in the midst, occupy not the place
    That is rightfully his by his own divine grace.
Put Christ in the midst and then there let him stay;
    He'll abundantly bless you as day succeeds day.

And when testings come, as most surely they will,
    Keep Christ at the centre, keep trusting him still.
He'll bring them to pass in his own given way,
    He'll strengthen you through them, his love to display.

Keep Christ in the midst, follow closely his Word;
    He'll bless you above all that ever you heard.
Keep Christ in the midst and let no one beside
    Take up what is his: let him wholly preside.

Lead me to the Rock

[Based on Psalm 61:2–3.]

Psalm 61:2–3:
'From the ends
of the earth I call
to you, I call as
my heart grows
faint; lead me
to the rock that
is higher than
I. For you have
been my refuge,
a strong tower
against the foe.'

Lead me to the Rock that is higher than I,
Through the darkened clouds let me arise;
Let me look on the face of the radiant One,
Let me bask in the warmth of His eyes;
Let me rest in the cleft that was wrought just for me
To protect me from evil and harms;
Lead me to the Rock that is higher than I,
My refuge from fear and alarms.

Lead me to the Rock that is higher than I,
Let me safe in its shelter abide;
I can rise up from this world's tempestuous seas
Through the strength of the One at my side;
Let me dwell in the shadow of One who is love,
Let me feel the great strength of his care;
Lead me to the Rock that is higher than I,
For my shelter and refuge are there.

Lead me to the Rock that is higher than I,
Its foundation is sure and approved;
Let me rest in him solely, for his tender love
Shall never be shaken or moved;
For my Lord is that Rock and that fortress divine,
For the Lord is my strength and my stay;
For my Lord is that Rock that is higher than I:
In him is my rest day by day.

Searching

[Based on Proverbs 2:1–5.]

Step by step the Lord has brought you
   To this very point of time,
Through each bright and darkened pathway,
   Through all hills and rocky climb;
Faithful has he been towards you,
   Guarded every step you've trod,
Shielded you from all that's harmful—
   Your faithful, loving, caring God.

As he leads you safely onward
   May you in his ways abide;
Storing his commands within you,
   To his truths your heart's applied.
Turn your ears unto his wisdom,
   To him for holy insight call;
Cry aloud for understanding,
   Seeing he is All in all.

Deep within the darkest recess
    Shines the silver, hid to view;
Only by the deepest searching
    Are treasures seen of varied hue.
Search for wisdom as for silver
    Deep within God's precious Word;
Seek his face in each endeavour,
    For none shall lead you like the Lord.

As you gather precious wisdom
    Like the silver from the mine,
May you store it deep within you,
    May it through your being shine;
Then, as you follow in God's leading
    You will understand his ways,
You will walk in righteous pathways,
    Singing with a heart of praise.

Proverbs 2:4–5:
'… and if you look for it [wisdom] as for silver and search for it as for hidden treasure, then you will understand the fear of the Lord and find the knowledge of God.'

Side by side

[Based on 1 Timothy 4:7–8.]

*1 Timothy
4:7–8:*
*'... train
yourself to
be godly. For
physical training
is of some value,
but godliness
has value for all
things, holding
promise for both
the present life
and the life to
come.'*

Side by side with Christ your Saviour
    May you daily walk with him;
Seeking guidance from the Master,
    Guard your heart from every sin.
Daily give your sole attention
    To his Word, to ceaseless prayer;
Then you'll know his precious presence
    To be with you everywhere.

Side by side, walk on together,
    Train yourself in godly ways;
Honour him with all your being:
    This will bring the Saviour praise.
Look to him in every hardship,
    Praise his Name, though tears would fall;
Look to him when joy's o'erflowing,
    Sound his praises over all.

Side by side, go, travel onwards
    To your sweet, celestial home,
There to be with Christ your Saviour,
    See his face—God's Holy One.
Daily walk your walk with patience,
    See that joy that's set before:
Side by side with Christ your Saviour,
    To live with him for evermore.

Unless

[Based on Matthew 7:18, 20.]

Matthew 7:18, 20:
'*A good tree cannot bear bad fruit, and a bad tree cannot bear good fruit …
Thus, by their fruit you will recognize them.*'

Unless we show how much we care
>To each and every one,
How can one know Christ's love is there
Within our hearts, unless we share
>God's only Son?

Unless the love of Christ abides,
>And we his fruit can see,
How can we know that one has cried
Unto the Lord, the crucified,
>And been made free?

Unless we love as Christ has loved,
>How can one simply know
That Christ indwells us from above?
That we are filled with heavenly love?
>Unless we show?

Unless that love of Christ is shown,
>How does one know there's care?
How does one know love's been made known
To those who say Christ's Name they own
>Unless they share?

Steps

[Based on 1 Timothy 4:7–12, 15–16.]

As you walk God's path before you,
As you seek his way ahead,
May you know that he is with you,
Guiding every step you tread.
Let no man then despise your youth
But walk on in the Saviour's truth.

Daily walking, seek his guidance
Through his Word, his precious Word,
Then before his throne, with boldness,
Bring your prayers before the Lord.
So train yourself in godly ways,
To bring the Saviour all his praise.

To believers all around you
May you an example be;
As they view your daily living
May they then your Saviour see.
And in like manner, those around
Will seek to make God's grace abound.

Watch your life and doctrine closely,
Do not then be led astray;
Persevere with Christ your Saviour,
He will lead you in his way.

    Devote yourself to him alone
    And glorify him on his throne.

So, dear one, Now the way's before you,
May you know our hearts' desire;
Follow on with Christ, our Saviour,
May your life to his aspire.

    Then we shall all united be
    With Christ, throughout eternity.

1 Timothy 4:12:
'Don't let anyone look down on you because you are young, but set an example for the believers in speech, in life, in love, in faith and in purity.'

Minor Prophets

Compassion

[Based on Jonah.]

Jonah 4:11:
'Should I not be concerned about that great city?'

F rom the voice of your calling, O Saviour,
  To the darkness of sin I would flee;
But your mercy and tender compassion
  Still pardon and sanctify me!
From the depths of deep darkness you've sought me,
  You've lifted me up to your side;
From the pit of destruction you've brought me
  By the measureless grace you've supplied.

Should I not then have likewise compassion
  On my fellow man, vile as I,
Who is lost in all sin's degradation,
  Who would hunger and perish and die?
Should I not then speak out the glad tidings
  Of salvation so rich and so free?
Should I not suffer all the deridings
  That arise from his sin, hurled at me?

Grant me, Lord, a much deeper compassion,
  To show out your love to all men;
To show them your mercy and pardon;
  To speak out salvation again!
Oh, let me not flee from your presence,
  But willingly go where you send,
To tell out to all—kings and peasants—
  The glory of salvation's end!

Dewdrops

[Based on Hosea 2:23; 14:1–9.]

Hosea 2:23:
*'I will show my
love to the one I
called "Not my
loved one."'*

O God of all faithfulness,
 Who pardons my sin,
  When in full repentance I turn;
Who heals all my waywardness,
Cleanses within—
  May I, of your ways, quickly learn.

With fragrance of cedar,
And blossom of flower,
  May your dew ever fall on my soul;
May my thoughts be discerning,
By your Spirit's power,
  And in righteous ways ever to stroll!

Downfall!

[Based on Obadiah.]

Obadiah 1:3:
'The pride of
your heart has
deceived you ...'

O boastful heart, so full of pride,
 The Lord is looking on,
Though you would mount on eagle's wings
  To make your lofty home;
Midst starry skies would build your nest
  And say, 'Who'll bring me down?'
The Lord of heaven is looking on
  And he will bring you down!

O boastful heart, sin's craggy rocks
  May be your hiding place
To shield your face from God above,
  But sin is not erased!
As you have done, those deeds all known
  Will fall upon your head!
And God will call account of all
  You've ever done or said!

Do not look down on others' lives
  And laugh them all to scorn;
Nor boast of morals tightly held
  Since the time when you were born.
Your deceitful ways are known to God
  And downwards you will fall;
Oh, turn to him, his mercy seek,
  The righteous Judge of all.

Focus

[Based on Habakkuk 1:2–4; 2:3–4.]

Habakkuk 2:4:
'... the
righteous will live
by his faith ...'

Do I lose sight of you, O God,
    When evil ways abound?
Oh, teach me, then, to look above
To see you on your throne of love,
    With sovereign glory crowned!

Help me to see the wider sphere
    Of your almighty plan;
Increase my faith that I may see
Your hand controlling all there be
    Within this world of man.

Lift me above these earthly plains
    Where I can sing your praise;
With heart of faith, Lord, let me live,
And in this way forever give
    My life through endless days.

Glory of salvation

[Based on Zechariah 6:12–13.]

own through the aeons of time, immemorial,
God's love shines out like a jewel in a crown,
Traced through the priesthood, a work mediatorial,
    Offers of praise to the highest renown!
Praise to the God who in deepest compassion
    Clothes poorest sinners with richest attire;
Clothes for his purpose in God-honoured fashion
    The sinner who's plucked as a brand from the fire!

Out of the Branch that will live on for ever
    Comes forth the fruit that will last for all time:
Sinners redeemed by salvation, unsevered,
    Sinners of earth from each nation and clime.
Built through the love of a sacrificed Saviour
    Into a temple not made by man's hands,
Worship will rise to the God of all favour,
    From those who follow the Father's commands!

Zechariah 6:12–13:
'Here is the man whose name is the Branch … It is he who will build the temple of the Lord …'

Immutable

[Based on Malachi 1:11; 3:6.]

Malachi 1:11:
'My *name will
be great among
the nations, from
the rising to the
setting of the
sun.'*

O changeless love, so infinite,
    O Name above all names,
How glorious is your throne above,
    Eternally the same!
Teach me your Name to love, revere,
    Its preciousness behold;
And may its presence in my heart
    For ever be extolled.

Your wondrous Name, high over all—
    Your people's great delight—
Shall in a coming day break forth
    And burst upon man's sight!
All praise shall rise to realms above
    And every knee shall bow;
The nations see your greatness then—
    The King of Glory now!

Incarnation

[Based on Micah 5:2–5.]

O f origin of old,
    Sent forth from ancient times,
The Ruler from on high—
Eternally sublime!
     His government shall know no end,
     The King of kings, the sinner's Friend.

Great Shepherd of the sheep,
In majesty arrayed,
Came forth to realms of time,
Was in a manger laid.
     Our peace he is, we live secure;
     His greatness reigns for evermore.

The Holy One of God—
Incarnate Deity—
Was born of virgin's womb
In meek humility!
     O mighty Ruler, come and reign
     Within those hearts that love your Name.

Micah 5:2:
*'But you,
Bethlehem
Ephrathah,
though you are
small among the
clans of Judah,
out of you will
come for me
one who will be
ruler over Israel,
whose origins are
from of old, from
ancient times.'*

Innermost

[Based on Joel.]

Rend your heart and not your garments,
    Search the very core within;
See your waywardness presiding,
    See the greatness of your sin!
God is full of all compassion,
    Gracious, full of tender love;
See the mercy of his pardon
    As you seek his face above.

Rend your heart and not your garments;
    Think not of the outward show.
God, he sees the inner being,
    Knows what no one else can know.
Even in the blackest darkness
    He his heavenly Light has sent;
Shows to you the depth of sorrow
    Brought by sin—its full extent!

Come, then, rend that heart within you,
    Come before God's throne on high.
Seek him with repentant sorrow;
    He will pardon, sanctify.
He can pour you out a blessing,
    For evermore a refuge be;
Rend your heart and not your garments,
    Receive God's peace eternally!

Joel 2:13:
'Rend your heart and not your garments. Return to the Lord your God, for he is gracious and compassionate, slow to anger and abounding in love, and he relents from sending calamity.'

Omniscience

[Based on Amos 3:3; 5:12, 24; 7:2.]

Amos 3:3:
*'Do two walk
together unless
they have agreed
to do so?'*

All-seeing eye with deepest search
That knows my every way,
What can I hide from your pure sight?
What can escape your piercing light
    That turns sin's night to day?

All-knowing God who can reveal
    The very heart within,
Whose justice, like a river, rolls
In judgement on the sinner's soul,
    Oh, wash my soul from sin.

I turn, Lord, in repentant faith,
    O Sovereign Lord, forgive;
So let me then in you abide,
We'll walk together side by side,
    And so for ever live.

Reconsider!

[Based on Zephaniah 2:1–3; 3:12, 17.]

Come, gather together, you nations of men,
Consider your ways and rethink them again!
The darkness of sin o'er your people resides,
    And God in his justice will chasten and chide.

You've sought not the Lord, neither called on his aid,
    Received not correction nor his voice obeyed;
His justice each morning brings light without fail,
    And measures out vengeance, with nought to avail!

Oh, seek now the Lord, all you meek of the land;
    Perhaps he will hide you in his gracious hand.
His justice will come, but you may escape all
    If you, in repentance, before his feet fall.

Your God then is with you, he's mighty to save,
    He's cleansed you within, all your sin he forgave;
You rest in his love, all your joy he restores,
    In gathering his own to be with him once more.

Zephaniah 3:12:
'But I will leave within you the meek and humble, who trust in the name of the Lord.'
v. 17: 'The Lord your God is with you, he is mighty to save. He will take great delight in you, he will quiet you with his love, he will rejoice over you with singing.'

Refuge

[Based on Nahum 1:15.]

Nahum 1:15:
'Look, there on
the mountains,
the feet of one
who brings
good news, who
proclaims peace!'

Have you not heard? Do you not know
You reap from your life whatever you sow?
For God on his throne will let nothing slip by,
He's holy and righteous, with all-seeing eye.

Your sins, they are many, and God does declare
That nothing escapes him; that all is laid bare!
And he will make end of your sin-given ways,
And call you to judgement for eternal days.

BUT

Have you not heard? Do you not know
That God is all-loving; to anger, he's slow?
For out on the mountains comes One with good news
That brings you his peace; that acquits the accused.

The Lord is so good, a refuge for you,
For his Son has paid all sin's penalty due.
So turn in repentance, and call now to him,
And he will grant pardon for all of your sin.

Reviewing!

[Based on Haggai.]

Haggai 1:5:
'*Now this is
what the Lord
Almighty says:
"Give careful
thought to your
ways."*'

O my soul, with countless labours
    Many are the hours I've spent.
Has it been for God's own glory?
    Is it all expedient?
Let me all my ways consider,
    Stand aside and view the scene;
Is it right God's work should suffer
    At my hands, at best, unclean?

Deep within my heart, I know it,
    Lies a ruin, all forlorn!
In my pleasure, oft forgotten,
    While I would my world adorn!
God's foundation lies deserted
    Of salvation, full and free!
Turn my heart and let me ponder
    How my life is going to be!

Lord, stir up my spirit in me,
    Guide me in your holy ways;
Build me up on your foundation
    Whereon I can offer praise.
Let me in my heart consider,
    Nought shall e'er give place to you;
Put aside all worldly pleasures,
    To give you all the glory due.

Focus

Anticipation

[Based on John 6:39–40; Romans 8:17–18, 25.]

Raised to life eternal,
Nevermore to die,
To be with Christ for evermore,
     To reign with him on high;
Oh, what a glorious truth is this—
To reign with him in heaven's bliss!

Joint heirs with Christ above,
     Partakers of his Name,
To share by grace his heavenly joys,
     Eternally the same;
There's nought on earth shall e'er divide
My life from his, the crucified!

Revealed in us supreme,
     The glory of the Lord;
For though we die, in him we live:
     Redemption is assured!
We patiently await the day
When he shall call us hence away!

John 6:40:
'For my Father's will is that everyone who looks to the Son and believes in him shall have eternal life, and I will raise him up at the last day.'

Complete in Christ

[Based on Colossians 2:9–10.]

To be at one with Christ
 Draws from my very breast
A depth of love as yet unknown,
 Its riches long possessed;
Cascading at his feet
 I gladly render all,
Poured out in humble plenitude
 To him, who gave his all.

At one with Christ, my Lord,
 My heart and his entwined,
Brings love from deep within my soul—
 A love that's unresigned.
May this for ever be,
 That I, in him complete,
May render him my humble all
 And worship at his feet.

Colossians 2:9–10:
 'For in Christ all the fulness of the Deity lives in bodily form, and you have been given fulness in Christ, who is the Head over every power and authority.'

Contrasts

[Based on Isaiah 40:26; Philippians 2:14–16.]

The far-flung starry host of space
    Has by God's hand been set in place,
And does his strength and power embrace;
Not one of them is missing!
    Each star is kept and called by name
    And would God's glory now proclaim,
    To spread abroad his matchless fame
    By thoughtful reminiscing.

And we, like stars, shine out so bright
Amid sin's darkest, blackest night,
And show forth God's eternal light—
Salvation's proclamation!
    We're called by name and kept by him
    To shine within this world of sin;
    Our light will never fade or dim
    Within our generation.

And so, shine out for all to see
From now unto eternity.

Daybreak

[Based on John 17:24.]

John 17:24:
  'Father, I want
those you have
given me to be
with me where
I am, and to see
my glory, the
glory you have
given me because
you loved me
before the
creation of the
world.'

Whene'er that blessed day shall break
  And shadows flee away,
When earthly mists shall quickly fade
  As night turns into day;
We then shall see eternal realms
  With Christ, our All in all;
No noontide bell its toll shall sound,
  No evening shadow fall.

And on that blessed, eternal day,
  Come, let us fix our gaze;
For fleeting is this world of time
  Enshrouded in sin's haze;
Come, let us look to Christ above,
  To Christ, our All in all,
As he dispels sin's darkest night,
  Our True Light over all.

Galilee

[Based on Mark 1:28.]

Mark 1:28:
'News about
him spread
quickly over the
whole region of
Galilee.'

O Galilee, your waters blue and glistening in the sun,
    If you could speak, what wonders you could tell of God's own Son;
O Galilee, your beauty far exceeds that seen by eye,
    For you have borne my Saviour and my Lord in days gone by.

O Galilee, I've trod your shores just as my Lord has trod,
    I've ridden on the gentle waves on which my Saviour stood;
O Galilee, I've seen surrounding hills and beauteous vales,
    And I have caught a freshened glimpse of him who bore the nails.

O Galilee, I cannot tell the wonders I have seen
    Within your shores—your waters—where my Saviour must have been;
But, oh, I see the beauty of my Lord with freshened eyes,
    I've seen the places where he walked and lived in lowly guise.

O Galilee, you've brought to me such views that none could tell,
    And I can praise my Saviour, which all other praise excels;
I thank God for the truths that lie within your golden shores,
    For having seen your beauty here, I'll praise my Saviour more.

For the joy

[Based on Hebrews 12:2.]

S et before us is the joy, all human thought
     transcending,
     A joy untouched by human hands unto
        our souls attending;
A gift from God—unmarred, unscarred—
        from his own hand extending,
     A perfect joy, by tongue untold, a joy that
        is unending.

And for this joy that's set before, so many men
        of old
     Stood firm upon the Word of God; midst
        tyranny, waxed bold.
Declaring all the truth of God, with courage
        they revealed it;
     Upheld by God's most gracious hand,
        with their own lives they sealed it.

For through those men a flame was lit that
        burns unto this day—
     A light outshining others in this world of
        dark decay;
They gave their lives that all may see the truth
        of God, the Saviour,
     And in this way they quelled the tongues
        of evil misbehaviour.

Of that joy, that perfect joy, I speak in this
  connection:
    Christ gave his life upon that cross,
      brought death into subjection;
His form was marred, so greatly scarred, to
  bring us to perfection;
    His joy is ours, and ours is his, by his own
      resurrection.

So, for the joy that's set before us, let our
  focus be
    To live for Christ whate'er may come
      from this world's tyranny!
Our suffering's for a little while; eternal is
  that joy
    That lies beyond this realm of time that
      nothing can destroy!

So, looking unto Jesus and for the joy that's set
  before,
    With boldness let us all endure, our love
      for him outpour;
For to see him as he is in that place beyond
  compare
    Is our joy to come but, better still, 'tis his
      that we are there!

Hebrews 12:2:
'Let us fix our
eyes on Jesus,
the author and
perfecter of our
faith, who for
the joy set before
him endured the
cross, scorning
its shame, and
sat down at the
right hand of the
throne of God.'

Light of his presence

[Based on Psalm 89:15; Psalm 76:4; 1 John 1:5, 7.]

1 John 1:5, 7:
'God is light; in him there is no darkness at all … if we walk in the light, as he is in the light, we have fellowship with one another, and the blood of Jesus, his Son, purifies us from all sin.'

Sin's darkness—'tis dispelled! Its shadows—all repelled!
> In light of God's own glory, all transcendent!
This light, unparalleled, has human thought excelled,
> In shining out in fullness, all resplendent!

No darkness can abide, no sinful way preside,
> For those whose walk is blameless in his presence!
For God shall be their guide—with nothing more beside—
> And they can walk with him in acquiescence!

God is eternal light, and would, with man, unite,
> To walk as one, as in the first creation;
And so sin's darkest night through Christ was put to flight,
> When justice met God's mercy in salvation.

If we walk in the light, as he is in the light,
> Our fellowship with each surpasses telling;
We'll see his glory bright in realms beyond the night,
> When he shall bring us home to his own dwelling.

Once, for all

[Based on Hebrews 9:11–28; Isaiah 53:6.]

Hebrews 9:12:
'… but he entered the Most Holy Place once for all by his own blood, having obtained eternal redemption.'

Once and for all, the great transaction's done!
    Secured upon Mount Calvary by God's own
    precious Son!
How rich redeeming blood once shed, how vast
    the ransom paid,
    When mercy met the wrath of God and all
    his love displayed!
Once and for all, sin's sacrifice is o'er,
    We stand redeemed in Christ, our Lord—in
    him, who's gone before!

Once and for all, salvation now is mine!
    Secured beneath the blood of Christ, my
    Saviour, all divine!
Now sprinkled on God's mercy seat—he has
    atonement made,
    For he has borne my punishment: on him my
    sins were laid.
Once and for all, he's entered heaven above,
    He's entered that Most Holy Place that I'm
    unworthy of.

Once and for all, my Saviour died for me!
    And I shall live and reign with him
    throughout eternity!

Peace beyond measure

[Based on Romans 5:1; Psalm 85:10; Philippians 4:7.]

God's inner peace—
  Beyond man's tongue to tell;
Too vast for minds to comprehend,
    Too strong for him to quell—
Resides within the hearts of those
    Who would his love proclaim,
And guards the very thoughts within
    Of all who trust his Name.

This inner peace—
    In righteousness now kissed—
Is shed within the sinner's heart,
    God's tender, loving tryst.
We stand alone within his grace,
    In faith here justified,
In Christ, who shed his precious blood
    Through love unquantified.

Romans 5:1:
'Therefore, since we have been justified through faith, we have peace with God through our Lord Jesus Christ.'

Precious promises

[Based on 2 Peter 1:3–4; 2 Corinthians 1:20.]

S uch great and precious promises
　　Reside in Christ our Lord,
That we might be at one with him,
　　For evermore assured.
Of every promise God has made
　　In Christ, each one is 'yea',
For he shall ne'er his love remove,
　　Nor faithfulness betray.

Of all his precious promises
　　Has any ever failed?
Has God recanted on his Word?
　　His benefits curtailed?
Our God is faithful to the end,
　　Unchanging in his ways;
A true and trusted anchor, he,
　　The source of all our praise.

2 Peter 1:4:
'Through these
he has given us
his very great
and precious
promises, so
that through
them you may
participate in
the divine nature
and escape the
corruption in the
world caused by
evil desires.'

Perfect care

[Based on 1 Peter 5:7; Isaiah 43:4.]

When clouds of storm o'erspread the skies,
Causing problems to arise,
Come, turn your thoughts to me, that thing to share;
When rough and steep appears the way,
Let your mind upon me stay,
And I will give you rest from that you bear.

From those things that burden you,
Remember, they concern me, too;
So, cast them onto me; I will sustain.
In your weakness, seek my might,
In Satan's battles, let me fight;
Come unto me and call upon my Name.

You're very precious in my sight,
Therefore it is my delight
To educate you, share in all you do.
In circumstances that prevail,
You will find I do not fail,
That I am here to help to pull you through.

When sorrowful and bowed with grief,
I am here to bring relief;
To comfort you, abolish every fear.
Has a close friend failed you?
There is a power available;
Leave it to me, and to myself draw near.

Of all your plans, have none worked out?
Is there trouble all about?
    Do you wonder why it could not be?
Let me arrange your plans for you,
For I know what is best for you;
    Don't be independent: trust in me!

Upon my words, come, set your heart,
And I my blessing shall impart
    If you will just trust me in everything.
I know it's hard, but you can do,
For I will give that strength to you;
    Release yourself, and wholly to me cling.

1 Peter 5:7:
'Cast all your anxiety on him because he cares for you.'

Reconciled!

[Based on 1 Peter 2:9–10; Romans 5:10–11; 2 Corinthians 5:17–21.]

Mercy's call came low and sweet
And bowed me at my Saviour's feet,
When I was made in him complete
    By his propitiation;
His blood once shed now cleanses me—
This soul steeped in iniquity—
And I am found at liberty
    Through reconciliation!

Once far from God, I now draw nigh
Through Jesus, to his throne on high;
For Christ has come my death to die,
    Procuring my salvation.
What wondrous truth in which I stand,
A sinner brought by God's own hand
To live there in Immanuel's land
    In ceaseless adoration!

1 Peter 2:9–10:
'But you are a chosen people, a royal priesthood, a holy nation, a people belonging to God, that you may declare the praises of him who called you out of darkness into his wonderful light. Once you were not a people, but now you are the people of God; once you had not received mercy, but now you have received mercy.'

Stability

[Based on James 1:17; Malachi 3:6.]

Upon my God, dependent
    I live, in him secure;
Within his love resplendent,
    Salvation shall endure.
Midst swirling waves of tempest
    He shall my anchor be,
Midst rising fears of unrest
    There's none as strong as he.

Within his hand, protected
    I bide, and none shall move;
In trials unsuspected
    I'm sheltered by his love.
Above, beneath, around me
    That love shall never fail;
His shadow, it surrounds me
    In every stormy gale.

Midst changing scenes assailing,
    My God shall constant be;
In all that is prevailing
    No change in him I see.
And though my faith may falter,
    Let this my portion be:
These truths—which do not alter—
    Henceforth will strengthen me.

James 1:17:
'Every good and perfect gift is from above, coming down from the Father of the heavenly lights, who does not change like shifting shadows.'

71

Renewed strength

[Based on Isaiah 40:31; 2 Corinthians 12:9.]

A rise, my precious soul, look up and spread
    your wings on high;
      Above this world's tempestuous seas soar up
        and glide and fly.
The Lord has given strength renewed to rise above
      the clouds,
      So rise, my soul, rise upward, for the Lord has
        heard your cry.

To those that trust in God's dear Name, he gives
      this strength renewed,
      A strength that had no knowing hitherto, with
        grace endued.
When we are at our weakest point, in gentleness he
      comes
      To lift above sin's darkness here, to rise
        towards the sun.

He knows your situation, he know your weakest
      points,
      He knows your faith is feeble, he knows when
        you are faint;
But often it is when you have no strength left of
      your own
      That he will come and minister, supplying of
        his own.

His strength is oh so mighty, made all perfect when
you're weak—
'Tis then that you will know it in its power, all
unique.
While trusting here within yourself, his strength
cannot be known,
So rest in him now, precious soul, absorb it all
alone.

Your strength shall be renewed as you commit your
all to him,
He lifts you up, protects you from the fears
that lurk within;
He fights the foe without for you—our Lord is all
you need—
So rise, my soul, rise upwards—he is all your
strength indeed.

Isaiah 40:31:
*'... but those
who hope in the
Lord will renew
their strength.
They will soar on
wings like eagles;
they will run and
not grow weary,
they will walk
and not be faint.'*

Steal not tomorrow

[Based on Psalm 31:14–15.]

Psalm 31:14–15:
'But I trust in you, O Lord; I say, "You are my God." My times are in your hands ...'

S teal not tomorrow out of the Father's hand,
For the time has not yet come to fulfil what he has planned;
Those moments are as precious as the many hours that pass,
But rest assured that, in his time, the answer comes at last.

God answers every prayer that a repentant sinner prays,
Yet it may not be the answer of our own desired way;
Sometimes it comes as 'No', and very often, 'Wait',
But no prayer goes unanswered that a true believer makes.

The precious school of patience he has called you to attend
To teach you there the meaning of an even better end.
He has not left you to endure without a cause in sight,
He knows that, by your waiting, you will learn his way is right.

And when that time has come when tomorrow is today,
And the answer's been revealed in the most diverse of ways,
Just thank the precious Father that he's ended all your sorrow
And spare a thought for someone who is praying for tomorrow.

Take hold

[Based on Philippians 3:13–14; James 1:12.]

Philippians 3:13–14:
'But one thing I do: Forgetting what is behind and straining towards what is ahead, I press on towards the goal to win the prize for which God has called me heavenwards in Christ Jesus.'

Press on! Press on towards the goal
 To gain the heavenly prize;
Forgetting what has gone before,
 Stand firm and say, 'Arise!'
Look far beyond the here and now,
 With godly grace pursue
The heavenly calling of your Lord,
 With every strength renewed.

Take hold upon the crown of life,
 If you would hold him dear,
Promised by God to those who through
 Life's trials persevere;
Look up! Look forward! Look beyond!
 See Christ upon his throne,
And see the joy that set's before,
 That's claimed you for his own.

Travelling companion

[Based on Matthew 28:20; Deuteronomy 31:6.]

Matthew 28:20:
'And surely
I am with you
always, to the
very end of the
age.'

As you tread the pathway of your pilgrim journey here,
Remember as you travel, 'tis the Lord that gently steers;
Remember, too, that others have the journey safely trod
    Led by none other than their Lord, their Saviour and their God.

So step by step we travel, just by faith and not by sight—
    We're looking unto Jesus to protect us by his might.
Step by step we follow while the Saviour leads us on
    To bring us safe to heaven, where our forerunners have gone.

Sometimes upon that journey far the pitfalls come along,
    And we would lie and softly weep as things have all gone wrong;
But Jesus Christ is there to lift us up and give us strength,
    To comfort us, to love us, to encourage us at length.

So when those pitfalls come and you are feeling all is lost,
    Your weaknesses have let you down, you cannot bear the cost,
Just look then unto Jesus; he will comfort and secure,
    Just as he has with others who have felt the worldly lure.

The Lord is strong and mighty and will gently lead you on,
    Will lift you up when you are down, will make the weakest strong;
Remember, there are others he has safely led before
    And brought them gently through to land upon that golden shore.

Unfathomed!

[Based on 1 John 3:1; 4:9–10.]

O h, depth of love divine,
      Unchanging in its source,
Unplumbed! Unfathomed! Unreserved!
      Unlimited in course!
Oh, who can know its ways?
      Or tell of all its might?
Its showers of rich and endless joys
      Cascade from heavenly heights.

Such depth of love divine,
      On sinners now bestowed,
Comes from the Father's throne on high
      Through Christ, who bore sin's load;
For he was crucified!
      Our sacrifice is he!
That we might live with him above
      Throughout eternity.

1 John 3:1:
'How great is the love the Father has lavished on us, that we should be called children of God! And that is what we are!'

Waiting

[Based on Psalm 37:7.]

Psalm 37:7:
*'Be still before
the Lord and
wait patiently for
him.'*

At his set time, child of God,
He makes known his perfect plan;
He reveals his path before you
    And will lead you by the hand.
At his set time, child of God,
    You must follow where he leads,
For his wisdom and his knowledge
    Are fulfilling all your needs
    Along the way.

In the meantime, child of God,
    When his plan is not yet known,
You must faithfully go forward
    Planting footsteps in his own.
In the meantime, child of God—
    Ways ahead seem hard and long—
He is faithful that has promised
    And you will not suffer long,
    Come what may.

At his set times and his meantimes,
    God is always in control;
He will give the grace you're lacking,
    Speaking peace unto your soul.
Follow on where'er he leads you,
    Trusting ever, trusting still;
'Til the time of the revealing
    Of his good and perfect will,
    Watch and pray.

Wings

[Based on James 5:16.]

James 5:16:
'The prayer of
a righteous man
is powerful and
effective.'

Borne on wings of deepest prayer
Unto the throne of grace,
The greatest strength in weakness sought
    Before the Father's face;
May you know his comfort, peace,
    His love beyond compare,
For you are held within his hand,
    Within his tender care.

Walk of wisdom

*[Based on Proverbs 8:6–36; also Proverbs 3:13–17;
4:10–12; 9:10.]*

Within the way of righteousness she walks
    with beauty beaming,
      Her pathways—like the early dawn with
      silvery light a-gleaming—
Break forth into a brighter day, with glory's
    splendour shining,
      Revealing all her pleasant ways with
      perfect peace combining.

From godly counsels she came forth—the first
    of all creation—
      To be God's craftsman at his side, with
      joyful admiration;
So blessed are those that keep her ways, who
    listen to her calling
      And follow in her straightened paths, thus
      keeping them from falling.

Her words are faultless, just and true, her
    paths are for our leading;
      Her counsels wise, her judgements sound,
      recorded for our heeding.
She loves the ones that love her name, and
    those that seek her find her;
      Her wealth bestowed a treasury fills of all
      who walk behind her.

Such worthy things she has to say to those who
 are discerning,
  To those who tread her lovely paths, who
  to her words have yearning;
For all her wealth is greater far than this
 world's fairest treasure,
  Beyond comparison of all, excelling
  earthly measure.

May you discover wisdom's path and follow
 in her leading,
  And learn of her in godly fear, in every
  way succeeding;
For all her worth is greater far than gold or
 choicest silver,
  For they will perish here in time, but
  wisdom lasts for ever.

*Proverbs
3:13–15:*
*'Blessed is the
man who finds
wisdom, the
man who gains
understanding,
for she is more
profitable than
silver and yields
better returns
than gold.
She is more
precious than
rubies; nothing
you desire can
compare with
her.'*

Christmas & New Year

Fulfilled!

[Based on Isaiah 9:6–7; Matthew 2:1–2.]

A child is born, a son is given:
Eternal God made man;
Here shines the everlasting Light
That shone e'er time began!
He low within the manger laid
Is cradled by a Hebrew maid,
According to God's plan.

Wonderful Counsellor is He,
The Mighty God, supreme!
Eternal Father, e'er the same;
No change in him is seen!
The everlasting Prince of Peace,
The King whose reign will never cease;
A Saviour to redeem!

Isaiah 9:6:
'For to us a child is born, to us a son is given, and the government will be on his shoulders. And he will be called Wonderful Counsellor, Mighty God, Everlasting Father, Prince of Peace.'

Crowning glory

[Based on Psalm 65:11.]

You crown the year with goodness, Lord,
 Your faithfulness unchanging;
Yet, as I go from day to day,
 My own life rearranging,
I fail to see, so many times,
 The fullness of your blessings,
Forget to bring you thankfulness
 For every good possessing.

Lord, as the purple morning breaks,
 And evening's red sky fades,
I see your hand of majesty
 In all that you have made:
I see your all-sustaining power
 Spread forth in all the earth,
Creation's song breaks out in joy
 To sound the Maker's worth.

And as I look back o'er this year,
 The countless things reviewing,
I see your strong, protective hand
 In all that I've been doing;
The good, the bad, the in-between,
 Those times when I have failed you,
Your faithfulness remained the same,
 Even when my sin had veiled you.

So as I travel day by day
    This new year fast approaching,
Cause me, O Lord, to look to you
    In all that I am broaching;
Your faithfulness is e'er the same,
    Your love? 'Tis never failing!
Help me, O Lord, to trust in you
    In all that is prevailing!

You've crowned this year with goodness, Lord
    My thanks to you I render;
Forgive my ever-weakening heart
    For failing to remember
That all I have has come from you,
    Your mercies? They're abounding!
So may my soul break forth in song,
    All praise to you resounding.

Psalm 65:11:
'You crown the year with your bounty, and your carts overflow with abundance.'

King of glory

[Based on Psalm 24; Micah 5:2; Matthew 2;
2 Corinthians 8:9.]

The King of glory comes!
The great Messiah reigns!
The Ruler over all the earth
Is Lord of each domain.
Come, see this King of glory now!
Majestic honours crown his brow!

And yet this King we see
Within a manger laid;
The eternal Son of God on high
In manhood now arrayed.
Come, see this King of glory now!
Humbly born on earth below!

His glory laid aside,
He dons humanity,
To dwell within this sin-torn world
In poorest poverty!
Come, see this King of glory now!
From riches unto rags brought low!

But why should this be so?
God's King made pauper here?
Why should he leave his heavenly throne
To dwell within earth's sphere?
It was that he God's love should show
By living with us here below.

This King of glory came
To pay the price of sin,
To live and die here as a man
To make us pure within;
His precious, royal blood was shed
By dying in the sinner's stead.

But see his glory now!
As, seated on his throne,
Once more he takes his rightful place
And wears the victor's crown!
For he has triumphed o'er the grave
In resurrection power, to save.

Lift up your heads and praise
Our King of glory now!
He ever lives and reigns supreme!
Before him let us bow.
As wise men came his face to seek,
So let us worship at his feet!

Who is this King of glory?
The Lord Almighty!
He is the King of glory!

*2 Corinthians
8:9:*
*'For you know
the grace of
our Lord Jesus
Christ, that
though he was
rich, yet for your
sakes he became
poor, so that
you through his
poverty might
become rich.'*

Salvation's dawn

[Based on Luke 2:8–20; 1 John 4:14.]

Rejoice! Rejoice! Salvation's dawn has broken!
Just as the word was spoken
   To prophets, as of old;
Messiah comes! Messiah comes!
   The longed-for promise given;
The Holy One of heaven,
The Holy One of heaven,
   Redemption's plan unfolds.

Rejoice! Rejoice! Join all the heavenly chorus!
   For God has brought before us
   Salvation's dawn, so bright;
In cradled arms, in cradled arms,
   The infant King of glory,
Theme of redemption's story,
Theme of redemption's story,
   Was born upon that night.

Rejoice! Rejoice! The shepherds came to seek him;
   They heard the angels speaking
   Glad tidings from the sky.
On bended knee, on bended knee,
   They humbly bow before him;
They worship and adore him,
They worship and adore him,
   The Son of God Most High.

Rejoice! Rejoice! Just see that star a-shining!

See God and man combining!

True manhood now is made.

The wise men came, the wise men came

With treasures all a-laden

To seek the lowly maiden,

To seek the lowly maiden,

And view her precious Babe.

Rejoice! Rejoice! Salvation's dawn has broken!

Just as the word was spoken

To prophets, as of old;

Messiah comes! Messiah comes!

The longed-for promise given;

The Holy One of heaven,

The Holy One of heaven,

Redemption's plan unfolds.

Luke 2:15–16:
'When the angels had left them and gone into heaven, the shepherds said to one another, "Let's go to Bethlehem and see this thing that has happened, which the Lord has told us about." So they hurried off and found Mary and Joseph, and the baby, who was lying in the manger.'

Nativity's reality

[Based on Luke 2:1–7; Matthew 2:22–23.]

As my feet have walked the land in which
    your feet have trod,
    As I have seen the sights you saw, the
      places where you stood,
I can but thank and praise you for the love
      you've shown to me
    In bringing me salvation by your death on
      Calvary.

And as we celebrate the time when you came
      here below,
    Help us to celebrate with joy, O Saviour;
    let us know
The truth that lies within the bounds of your
      nativity;
    Help us believe that truth, O Lord, in its
      reality.

Luke 2:6–7:
'While they were there [in Bethlehem in Judea], the time came for the baby to be born, and she gave birth to her firstborn, a son. She wrapped him in cloths and placed him in a manger, because there was no room for them in the inn.'

Matthew 2:22–23:
'But when he [Joseph] heard that Archelaus was reigning in Judea in place of his father Herod, he was afraid to go there. Having been warned in a dream, he withdrew to the district of Galilee, and he went and lived in a town called Nazareth. So was fulfilled what was said through the prophets: "He will be called a Nazarene."'

Coming soon

When Heaven calls your name
People in the Bible who heard God speak

ROGER ELLSWORTH

128PP, PAPERBACK

ISBN 978-1-84625-102-3

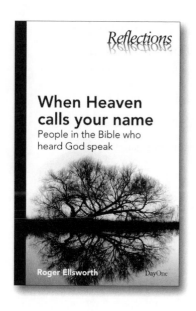

Believing that repetition indicates emphasis, Roger Ellsworth examines occasions in the Bible in which God the Father or God the Son repeated someone's name. He asserts that these instances were meant to make certain truths 'dance' before our eyes. In an increasingly difficult and challenging world, these truths will thrill, comfort and guide all those who genuinely embrace them.

'God speaks. He has spoken, and he continues to speak today. Through these vivid portraits of Heaven's calls, you will overhear the voice of God speaking specifically and clearly to you.'

TODD BRADY, PASTOR OF THE FIRST BAPTIST CHURCH OF PADUCAH, KENTUCKY

They echoed the voice of God

Reflections on the Minor Prophets

ROGER ELLSWORTH

128PP, PAPERBACK

ISBN 978-1-84625-101-6

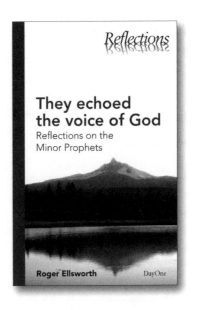

Many carry a little Bible and believe in a little God. Their Bibles are little because they ignore so many of its books. Their God is little because they ignore so many of the Bible's truths. The Minor Prophets can help us. These men made sense of their circumstances and found strength for their challenges by basking in the God who was above it all and in it all. The God they served was wise enough to plan and strong enough to achieve. This study of their messages will help us have both bigger Bibles and a bigger God.

'Roger Ellsworth helps us appreciate how the so-called Minor Prophets make known the character and work of our great God. This book is a great introduction to and overview of their prophecies. Read it to become acquainted with these sometimes overlooked servants and, more importantly, with the unchangeable God whose message they proclaimed.'

TOM ASCOL, DIRECTOR OF FOUNDERS MINISTRIES AND PASTOR, GRACE BAPTIST CHURCH, CAPE CORAL, FLORIDA

'Laced with helpful, practical application, this book shows how each prophet emphasized a particular aspect of God's character, giving an overall picture that is compelling.'

JIM WINTER, MINISTER OF HORSELL EVANGELICAL CHURCH, WOKING

Coming soon

Under God's smile
The Trinitarian Blessing of
2 Corinthians 13:14

DEREK PRIME

128PP, PAPERBACK

ISBN 978-1-84625-059-0

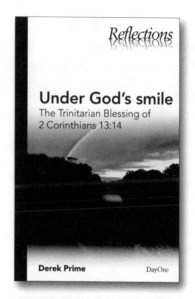

During recent decades, it has become the practice of Christians in many churches and in university and college Christian Unions to commit one another to God's grace and care with the words 'May the grace of the Lord Jesus Christ, and the love of God, and the fellowship of the Holy Spirit be with us all' (2 Corinthians 13:14). They are familiar words, but what do they actually mean? For what are we praying?

So that we do not repeat these words without appreciating their full implication, Derek Prime explores them and considers the three Persons of the Trinity in their different, yet perfectly harmonious, relationship to every believer. Written in an easy-to-read style, this book is thoroughly rooted in the Scriptures and is a demonstration that solid biblical truth is both heart-warming and exciting.

'Wholesome food for the average Christian reader and devotional writing of the highest order'
EVANGELICALS NOW

'An easily-read book, helpful in all stages of Christian life'
GRACE MAGAZINE

'Derek Prime's ministry is much appreciated by many Christian groups, including ourselves. Like all his other books … biblically based and easy to read'
ASSOCIATED PRESBYTERIANS NEWS

'If, like me, you are constantly on the lookout for books that say a great deal in short order, you will be delighted by what you hold in your hand. It is a special gift not only to expound what the blessing of the triune God means, but also to explain why it matters. We have come to expect this from Derek Prime, and once again he hits the mark.'
ALISTAIR BEGG, SENIOR PASTOR, PARKSIDE CHURCH, CHAGRIN FALLS, OHIO

About Day One:

Day One's threefold commitment:

- To be faithful to the Bible, God's inerrant, infallible Word;
- To be relevant to our modern generation;
- To be excellent in our publication standards.

I continue to be thankful for the publications of Day One. They are biblical; they have sound theology; and they are relevant to the issues at hand. The material is condensed and manageable while, at the same time, being complete—a challenging balance to find. We are happy in our ministry to make use of these excellent publications.

JOHN MACARTHUR, PASTOR-TEACHER, GRACE COMMUNITY CHURCH, CALIFORNIA

It is a great encouragement to see Day One making such excellent progress. Their publications are always biblical, accessible and attractively produced, with no compromise on quality. Long may their progress continue and increase!

JOHN BLANCHARD, AUTHOR, EVANGELIST AND APOLOGIST

Visit our web site for more information and
to request a free catalogue of our books.

www.dayone.co.uk